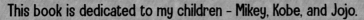

Ninja Life Hacks™

I LOVE YOU, Little Ninja

Ninja Life Hacks

By Mary Nhin

You lie on the ground, you roll around,
Tears are in your eyes.
You laugh so hard I think you'll burst!
Now **that** would be a surprise!

You live to give, you care and share,
It's such a lovely trait.
But then what happens when **you** feel down?
And **you're** not feeling too great?

When you feel lonely,
And your friends are not around,
You understand and know that
There's still fun to be found.

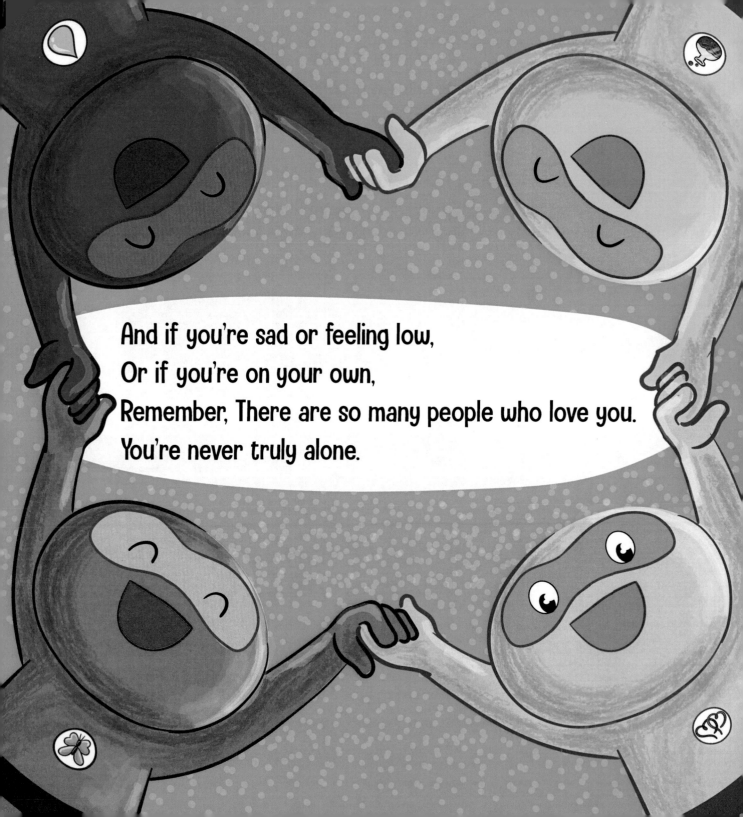

And if you're sad or feeling low,
Or if you're on your own,
Remember, There are so many people who love you.
You're never truly alone.

I love to hear from my readers. Email me your feedback or thoughts on what my next story should be at growgritpress@gmail.com

Yours truly, Mary

 @marynhin @GrowGrit
#NinjaLifeHacks

 Ninja Life Hacks

 Mary Nhin   Ninja Life Hacks

 @ninjalifehacks_tv

Made in United States
North Haven, CT
10 February 2023

32324623R00018